More Time to Grow

More
Time to
Grow

Explaining Mental Retardation
to Children: A Story

————— ✳ —————

SHARON HYA GROLLMAN

*with a Parents' and Teachers' Guide
by Robert Perske*

Illustrated by Arthur Polonsky

Beacon Press
Boston

Beacon Press books are published under the auspices
of the Unitarian Universalist Association

Simultaneous publication in casebound and paperback editions

Published simultaneously in Canada by
Fitzhenry & Whiteside Limited, Toronto

Printed in the United States of America

(hardcover)   9 8 7 6 5 4 3 2 1
(paperback)   9 8 7 6 5 4 3 2 1

Grateful acknowledgment is made to Abingdon Press for
permission to reprint material from *New Directions for
Parents of Persons Who Are Retarded* by Robert Perske
(Nashville: Abingdon Press, 1973).

Library of Congress Cataloging in Publication Data

Grollman, Sharon Hya
    More time to grow.
    Bibliography: p.
    SUMMARY: An illustrative story accompanies questions
and activities for children, a guide for parents and
teachers, and a list of recommended resources on mental
retardation.
    1. Mental deficiency — Juvenile literature [1. Mentally
handicapped].   I. Polonsky, Arthur.   II. Title.

RC570.G755   618.9′28′588   76–48513
ISBN 0–8070–2370–1
ISBN 0–8070–2371–X (pbk.)

For My Parents

Contents

What This Book Is About

Say the phrase "mental retardation." It conjures up all kinds of images. Yet adults—parents and teachers—should be able to handle this reality of life. If you are having difficulty with the subject, think of your children. They see people who look and act differently. "Strange, aren't they? Something must be wrong with them." Which means, "I don't understand." And since they don't understand, they throw out the expression, "That person's a retard."

How you can explain this difficult subject to children is the subject of this book. Through the story, one gains insight into the world of the mentally retarded. But the book does not end there.

There are "Questions to Think About" which challenge you to become aware not only of the characters' feelings, but of your own reactions toward exceptional people.

The "Activities for Children" section encourages further exploration into the lives of individuals with special needs as children act out various scenes and situations.

Robert Perske's "Guide for Parents and Teachers" suggests ways to utilize the book more effectively as it helps you, the adults, to better comprehend the subject.

Finally, there is a comprehensive, annotated list of organizations, books, and films which can lead you and your children to a deeper understanding of individuals who need more time to grow.

I wish to thank Ora Stevens, the teacher who welcomed me into a classroom filled with very special children: Howard, Pam, Kevin, Alfonso, Dominique, Susan, Lisa, Tonino, David, Chris, Clem, and Chipper.

—*Sharon Hya Grollman*

More Time to Grow

Nine-year-old Carla and her five-year-old brother, Arthur, sat in the garden—Carla with her new puzzle, Arthur with his crayons and coloring book.

1

"Shh," and Carla motioned with her hand for Arthur to stop humming. Then, looking up, she whined, "You're not supposed to color outside the lines, silly." The way she said it, drawing the words out, made Arthur laugh.

"What's so funny?" she asked, trying to keep a straight face, but a giggle crept up her throat.

4

"You," he mumbled, and he scribbled orange and red crayon all over the page because it made Carla laugh. And every time she started to look serious again, he scribbled another page.

Suddenly Carla stood up and yelled, "Arthur, are you crazy or something?" Bending down, she gathered the pieces of her puzzle with one hand, and with the other she made a fist as if she were going to hit him, but she didn't.

For a moment she looked at the pieces
of the puzzle covered with newly made
crayon marks. Again she spoke, her voice
tight with anger, "Arthur, how could you
do that? My new puzzle . . ."

Arthur looked up at her, his smile fad-
ing into a frown.

"I was only playing," he said, and he repeated the words over and over so that they sounded like music, going up and down with his sobs.

Carla stamped away, taking three deep breaths because that always made her feel a little less angry.

She wanted to understand Arthur. He was fun sometimes, but then he always did such stupid things. Mommy said he needed more time to grow than other children. But he was different. He didn't have any friends. He couldn't tie his shoelaces. He wasn't any good at kickball. He couldn't even color right. And . . . "Why does he have to be my brother?" she thought. Then Daddy's words, "Be patient" rang in her head and again she felt angry—not at Arthur, but at herself.

11

The house had seemed different ever since Arthur went to the doctor. Mommy's eyes were red a lot and Daddy looked so tired. Sometimes they locked their door, and they would whisper so softly that Carla couldn't hear their words, even when she held her breath.

When she asked them what was wrong, they put on a smile that looked more sad than happy and answered, ''Nothing, honey.''

15

It made her lonely because she felt left out. It was almost as if it weren't her home anymore, as if she were in the wrong place. Sometimes the house didn't even look the same.

And she felt more private. Because now she kept all her thoughts to herself, and there were so many feelings that it felt like a knot growing inside her stomach.

Then one day Mommy and Daddy asked Carla to take a walk. That's what they did when they talked about important things.

Carla spoke first. "Is Arthur okay?" Her voice squeaked and it surprised her, almost as if the noises weren't coming from her.

Daddy answered, "He's——" and he took her hand, "retarded."

16

17

The sound of the word made something hurt inside Carla—not really in her body, more inside that knot of feeling. She didn't understand, even though she'd heard the word before. Sometimes at school the kids called someone a "retard" if he did something wrong, something stupid. She knew it was a bad word. And it buzzed in her head, making her dizzy. And she got angry at Arthur because he was retarded. It was because of him that everyone was unhappy.

Once she even saw Daddy crying. Then she felt afraid. Was it all her fault somehow?

And she remembered the times she'd wanted to hit Arthur, to hurt him, to make him disappear.

When she heard Mommy's voice she
was surprised. She had forgotten that she
was walking, that it was spring and the flowers and trees were budding, that she wasn't
alone. "Do you know what retarded
means?"

20

Carla almost blurted out "stupid" but she didn't.

So they told her that it meant different. Not worse, but different. "He will learn and grow more slowly than you and your friends. We'll have to help him more," Daddy said. "But don't think we love you any less. You'll always be very special to us."

21

Carla bit her lip to hold back the tears. "Well . . . why then?" and with her words, tears came. "Why did it have to happen to us? If only I'd been nicer to him," she muttered.

22

"You didn't cause it. Nothing you did made Arthur——"

But Mommy didn't finish because Carla interrupted, "Maybe the doctor was wrong. Maybe he made a mistake. Maybe Arthur will get better. Maybe he just needs more time to grow——" And Carla's mind kept exploding with more maybe's, more if's.

"Arthur is retarded," Daddy said quietly.
"We don't understand it all either, but it's
okay to have our feelings, to talk about
them. To help Arthur. To help each other."

24

Arthur seemed different now. Not that
he acted differently. In fact, he was the
only one who didn't change. But he was
retarded, and to Carla he was as strange as
the word.

She stopped asking him to go to the drugstore, and she never visited him in the garden. But through her bedroom window she watched him playing with the sunlight, making rabbit ears with his fingers.

Other times he would just sit on the grass
and stare at the flowers.

Carla hadn't gone to the drugstore since
Mom and Dad told her about Arthur. When
she finally did, Sam, the man behind
counter asked, "Carla, how you doing?
Missed you."

"I'm okay," she answered, shrugging her shoulders.

"What's wrong? You don't have a smile for me today? How's Arthur?"

"All right, I guess."

"Carla?" and he motioned with his finger for her to come to the counter. Then he leaned over and with his other hand, which he'd been holding behind his back, he gave her a candy bar—her favorite kind.

31

Carla didn't say anything. She smiled.

Then Sam talked so softly that Carla squinted her eyes and put her head up close to his.

"Carla, you know I have a daughter.
She's very special. We go to the shore
together and every time we go she finds
something new.

"I've learned to notice things—the way
the tide comes in, how it feels when the
water touches my feet. Now, when I close
my eyes, I can feel the water. I know its
sounds.

"She taught me that. She's different from other kids. She'll never learn some things that they can do, but she's special. And you know what, Carla?"

She didn't say anything but raised her eyebrows waiting for him to answer.

"She's retarded."

"Really?" Carla mouthed, but no sounds came out.

"Really."

Carla sat by her bedroom window and took three deep breaths, not because she was angry, but because she was scared. Then, she knocked on her window so many times that her knuckles hurt. Slowly, Arthur turned his head up toward her and smiled. Carla smiled back.

When she went outside he was singing,
so she sat next to him and listened. When
he finished his song she asked where he
learned it.

"Made it up," he answered.

She laughed because she was surprised. Arthur laughed because he was happy. So he taught her his song and together they sang until their throats were dry, and then they sang some more. After a while, they just sat without saying anything.

When Mommy and Daddy came out, they sat down too, and smiled at Arthur —who was smiling at Carla—who was smiling at them.

Questions to Think About

Have you ever met anyone who reminded you of Arthur?

How did you feel?
Carla was afraid. Were you afraid like Carla?

Sometimes people laugh. Why do you think they would laugh?

Do you think Arthur would know if you made fun of him? How would he feel? How do you feel when people make fun of you? Does it hurt inside?

How do you think Carla would feel if you called Arthur names? How would you feel if someone called your brother or sister names?

They say that Arthur is different.

Have you ever felt that you were different from your friends?

What kinds of thoughts went through your head?

Maybe you acted strangely—or did you pretend you were the same as they were?

How did people act toward you?

How did you want them to act toward you?

Retardation is a broad term with many meanings; no one is exactly like Arthur. He is not exactly like other children who may be called retarded.

Does that word "retarded" frighten you?

Carla acted differently toward Arthur when her parents told her that he was retarded. Suddenly he seemed strange. Do you think he really changed?

Carla was angry. At whom?

What do you do to make yourself feel better when you are angry? Does talking about it help?

How could you have helped Carla during this time?

Would you like to know more about people who are called retarded? If you are interested, the following suggested activities, books, and films could help you learn more about this important subject.

Activities for Children

A SHORT INVITATION INTO THE WORLD OF DIFFERENCES

You have met Arthur and Carla. Now you have a chance to understand them better. How? By imagining how you would feel if you were in their position.

For all the activities that follow you might like to work with a parent or teacher. You can act out the scenes with friends, or just close your eyes and think about how you would react in the various situations.

Pretend you are Arthur and . . . During recess, a group of kids are playing basketball. You ask if you can join them. One team captain laughs, "Not on my team. I don't want to lose because of you."

The other captain doesn't even look at you when he says, "Scram, retard."

Nobody wants you to be on his team. How does it feel to be left out? What thoughts go through your head? Maybe you are angry at the team because they won't let you play with them. Because you're retarded, they won't even give you a chance.

They say you're not good enough, that you'll make the team lose. How does that make you feel about yourself?

LEARNING

Pretend you are Carla and . . . You want
to teach Arthur to tie his shoelaces. When
you tell your friends they shrug their
shoulders and laugh, "Don't waste your
time. He can't learn anyway!"

When your friends tell you that
Arthur can't learn, do you believe them or
do you try anyway?

Why would it be so important to
teach Arthur to tie his shoes? How would
you feel about Arthur if he accomplished
the task? How would you feel about
yourself?

Pretend again: Perhaps you are unable to
learn quickly. No matter how hard you try
in school, you never seem to get
anywhere. Your teacher and your mother
have a conference and you've been asked
to stay.

"Well, he does have some problems
in math," your teacher says.

"But he does his homework every night." Your mother repeats your words as if you had never said them.

"I try," you answer.

The teacher doesn't look at you. She responds, "I know he does try very hard, but . . ."

When you speak it's almost as if they don't hear you, as if you weren't even there. How does it feel?

Do you continue to speak or sit back and think about something else? What could you do to make them recognize you?

Try out the different ways, paying attention to how they respond.

DIFFERENCES IN LEARNING

No two people learn in the same way. Think about your friends. They may learn faster than you in science, though they can never do their math problems no matter how hard they try. They may be better softball players than you, while you are always the first to be picked for the kickball team.

Look around. There are differences everywhere. Each person learns and grows in a special way.

JOY IN LEARNING

Although Arthur happens to be retarded, he *can* grow and learn and feel good about it.

Can you remember how you felt when you wrote your name for the first time? Or baked your first cake all by yourself? Or hit your first home run?

Arthur, like you, may experience joy in learning.

Imagine that your class is working on multiplication problems. Somehow the numbers don't make sense to you. The other kids are solving difficult problems easily while you don't know where to begin with the simple tables. Maybe you feel like giving up.

How do you think you will react when you finally find the answer to a problem that once seemed impossible? Though you are behind the class, you have moved ahead.

You, like Arthur and other people who are retarded, can feel good about the steps you take in learning, no matter how small they may be.

Arthur may be different from you because he is retarded. But can you think of ways in which you are both alike?

People are alike in some ways and different in others. People called "retarded" learn and grow more slowly than others their age. Sometimes they look and act different as well. But although they have things in common, they are also very different from one another.

Think about this: Because you are a student, you are like other students. You all go to school. You all learn certain subjects.

But are you exactly like all other students? Do you all act the same way? Do you all like the same things?

You are similar to all students; yet you are different. While Arthur, too, is like other children who are called retarded, he is also different from them in his own way.

Make stories into plays and act them out:
- Write a story about a town where there are no differences, where everyone looks, acts, and believes the same way.
- Make up a story about a character who looks and acts very different. How do you react? Do you avoid him or try to learn more about him? Can you be friends?

OTHER DIFFERENCES

We have talked about people labeled retarded. There are also people who have other kinds of problems. Some cannot see, hear, speak clearly, or move their bodies easily. Now you can explore how people live with—and learn from—their differences.

What Is It Like to Be Blind?

Cover your eyes with a scarf. Hold a friend's hand as he leads you.

Pay attention to your different senses. Do they become more important?

How do you feel when cars pass you? Does your body become tense?

You are depending on your friend. He becomes important, not just someone to talk with. Right now you need him. How does it feel to need someone?

What do you do if he starts to run? Is it hard to keep up? Maybe you will bump into something, or trip.

He doesn't tell you there is a step, or a curve. Do you still trust him? Or do you begin to rely on your own feet, your own senses? Take turns.

. . . or be without arms?

Many people don't have arms or legs, or they can't use them because they have no control over their muscles.

Imagine how it would be if you could not use your hands. How could you play baseball or do activities that seem so simple like brushing your teeth, getting dressed, or eating a meal?

Some people who can't use their arms learn to rely on other parts of their body. Some have become artists by painting with their feet.

Try it. Put a pencil between your toes and try to write your name.

Tie one arm behind your back and continue your daily activities at home. How does it feel?

. . . or be unable to speak clearly?

Clean a small rubber ball and put it in your mouth. (Make sure it is big enough so you can't swallow it.) Try talking. Is it hard to pronounce the words?

Call someone you don't know very well, but don't explain what you are doing. How does the person react?

Pretend that you can never speak clearly, even when you don't have a rubber ball in your mouth. Your words stick together and sometimes people have to listen very carefully to understand what you are saying.

Your class is having a spelling contest. You and another person are the only students left standing. It is your turn. Your will win a prize if you give the right answer.

When the teacher gives you the word, your voice is more shaky than usual, and the sounds are stuck in your throat. Classmates begin to laugh. Your teacher, with a nod of the head, remarks, "Can't you speak more clearly?"

When you try again, the teacher interrupts and asks the other person for the answer. You lost the contest though you knew your answer was right.

How do you feel about yourself? How would you have handled the situation if you were the teacher?

THINGS TO DO

Have a party . . .

crafts day, or sports day with kids from a "special ed" class. Before your class plans an event, it may be helpful to invite a speaker from your local Association for Retarded Citizens. The speaker could further explain what mental retardation is and suggest other activities you could do to meet people who happen to be retarded.

After each event, talk about it. What did you expect? Were you afraid? Do you now feel differently about retarded people? How are they like you?

If there is a special ed class in your school, perhaps you can set up times to work in the classroom as teacher's helpers and as friends.

. . . or form your own club

Eight years ago, in Sweden, the first small youth club was formed in which half the members were "normal" and the other half "retarded." Each person was accepted for who he was, and each gave to the group what he could. Meetings were held, plans discussed, and *everyone* helped make decisions. Some of the activities included: going to restaurants and movies, having field trips, and putting on plays.

If you are interested, talk to your friends and make new friends with people who are called retarded. Discover what you can all create together!

A Guide for Parents and Teachers

by Robert Perske

Many persons in communities around the world are changing their minds about mentally retarded persons, how they should be treated, and where they should live. Once they were expected to live "off to the side" in protected, segregated institutions. Now, more and more people believe they should live within the regular flow of community life.

● They should live at home with special supports being provided for that home.

● They should be "mainstreamed" in the regular schools with special classes and resource teachers as needed.

● They should be allowed to be another "kid on the block." Why not? All of the other kids on the block are different from each other, and it's their differences that can give zest to truly healthy relationships.

There's no doubt about it. If this *is* a new direction society has begun to take, then the story of Carla, Arthur, and their parents—and other stories like it—will provide the catalyst for the new learning that can take place in all of us. It will be a hopeful sign for our communities when such handicapped persons can live in the middle of things with us as our relatives and neighbors.

This section is aimed at helping parents to be ready for stimulating discussions with their children regarding retarded brothers, sisters, or classmates. It's also intended to serve as a help for teachers who may see a chance to use it with their students. However, children do not respond on command, and one should never assume to know how children will respond in any situation. It's *their* growth we seek to reinforce, when *they* are ready. Wise parents and teachers learn to wait for proper moments. Here's hoping what is said here will help big persons to be ready to assist littler persons to understand and accept retarded persons.

How the Story May Be Used

After young children have read *More Time to Grow*, some of the following could take place:

- In a large group or class, some may want to ask questions and discuss it right away.

- With one or a few children, there may be no immediate response.

- Some of the most meaningful clarifications and discussions may come later, at a time when one or more children feel free to ask or give an opinion about a certain happening in Carla's experience.

- It can be pointed out that there is no neat or perfect way to solve such a problem, so children can be asked what they would have done if they had been in Carla's place, or the mother's, or the father's, or even Arthur's.

- The story could be read again. Children often like to hear the same story more than once.

- The adult, in a natural way, without overcontrolling the process, can be ready with a wide variety of *clarifications*, and he or she can point out *actions*

they may or may not choose to carry out. The best
learning processes come when children learn something they never knew before and they are inspired
to "do something" with such knowledge.

"More Time to Grow"

Gerda Klein, in her book *The Blue Rose,* describes
retarded Jenny as a "bird with shorter wings." Arthur is like
that. He will work for a longer time to achieve certain things
that Carla could master easily. Nevertheless, the title "More
Time to Grow" implies correctly that growth *can* take place.
Arthur—like us—has something coded deep in his life, an
urge to unfold and stretch for higher things. The only things
that can limit or snuff it out are certain forms of degenerative
illnesses or prejudiced reactions from others unable to
understand and accept him.

We have finally come to accept retarded persons as
developmental human beings. That means that as sure as
you have your own road map and rate of growth that is
different from everybody else's, so mentally retarded persons have theirs. In another book for parents* I described it
as follows:

"There was a day when I wanted to be like Willie Mays.
But it didn't take long for me to find I didn't have his road
map or rate of growth. Later, I wanted to be a Paul Tillich.
Didn't have his road map or rate either. So it finally dawned
on me that I had my own directions coded deep within my
humanity. It is my strong belief that the highest human dig-
nity and the greatest joy of living come from developing into
the best Bob Perske I can become with the givens I've got.
You can know that joy, too. So can your son or daughter!

*Robert Perske, *New Directions for Parents of Persons Who Are Re-
tarded* (Nashville: Abingdon Press, 1973), pp. 22, 23.

"What fools we've been in the past. We've imposed *our* limits on persons who have been labeled mentally retarded. We've said, 'They can't learn.' And then through society's ignorance and need to segregate them, they were forced to live within the limits we prophesied for them. In a sense, a child is lucky to be born at this period in history. You are lucky, too. Because of the developmental principle, there will be less shock and trauma in your life."

The words "more time to grow" imply that even small gains in Arthur's life can be like gold. "The child who is retarded has such a struggle to move from his crib to live, move, and adapt in the world, that each gain is a tremendous thing to him and his family. These small gains are important. For example:

- When a child learns to sit up in his crib, he can raise his intellectual functioning and adaptation at a tremendous rate. The ceiling isn't half as stimulating as watching everything that goes on around him.

- If the child can crawl, he can move about in his world and explore more things. Again, he can increase his functioning and adaptation at a tremendous rate.

- If a child can learn to walk, bingo! He can really move about in the world. If he learns to run, it's even better (although there will be times when you will doubt this).

- If he can be toilet trained, he has gained a real milestone in our society. Now he's ready to travel farther and learn much more.

- If he learns to feed himself, clothe himself, and take care of his own teeth, hands, and face, how proud everyone in the family can become.

- If he learns to come in out of the rain, he can be trusted even further. He can feel proud.

● If he can talk and ask for things, offer things, or express himself—both likes and dislikes—he reaches the high status of being a verbal communicator!

"In normal children you will take all this for granted. But you won't with a retarded child. Every gain is important. It amounts to what can be called *survival learning.* In one family, everyone made it his task to help little Joe develop. And each gain little Joe made was cause for a party. This father used to say, 'We celebrate the darnedest things at our house.'

"The small gains do not stop in early childhood. They continue throughout the life of the mentally retarded person. It is still a cause for celebration when a retarded person learns to ride the bus alone, proves he can hold down a job washing dishes, builds up his own savings account, buys his own television, maintains a rented room, pays his own income tax, attends church, or *chooses* to sit up with a sick friend."

Big Sister, Little Brother

Since I was a little brother, it's only fair to remind you that big sisters have *strong needs* to prove that little brothers are noxious little asses who are stupid and should be done in. Quite often their first intellectual graspings of the problem of evil emerge in such phrases as "Why does he have to be my brother?" Carla may be a good kid and all that, but she's growing. In a sense, she's "upwardly mobile," and such persons have little use for fumbling, inept "little people" as they attempt to master a society and a status—in this case adulthood—which is still above them. Therefore, parents and teachers, you must develop a canny sense about when the Carlas are angry at their little brothers for being retarded and when they are—I think normally—angry because little brother is little brother. As one who survived such an arrangement, I can tell you there is a difference.

Crayon marks on Carla's puzzle.
"Arthur, how could you do that?"

Easily. All little children try hard to do the right thing, but so often it turns out wrong. Growing up means developing good judgment about what one does in a certain situation. Coloring on Carla's puzzle may be normal faulty judgment, or it may hint at a slight delay in the development of proper judgment. Parents and teachers could discuss which it is with small children.

"She wanted to understand Arthur. . . .
But he was different. He didn't have any
friends. He couldn't tie his shoelaces. He
wasn't any good at kickball. He couldn't
even color right."

It would have been good if Carla did understand why
Arthur was different. It would have been better if she under-
stood much earlier than this. Discussions could arise
about actual retarded brothers, sisters, or neighbors, and
what barriers have kept them from keeping up with the rest.

In a series of integrated day care units in Omaha,
Melody Henn* has documented on film and in writing the
remarkable, nonprejudicial acceptance of "delayed" children by the so-called "normal" ones, because the
teachers and parents explain *why* Jenny can't walk, *why*
Jimmy can't talk, *why* Richard moves his arms in a wild
pattern. Melody has proved conclusively that an attractive,
well-functioning child can be friends with a not-so-attractive
child with grotesque leg braces and strange behavior, if the
adults are alert to answer questions about why the child
can't function better.

*For further information, write to Eastern Nebraska Community Of-
fice of Retardation, Omaha, Nebraska 06114.

"It made her lonely because she felt left out."

Brothers and sisters need every chance to express how they feel about their place in the family system. Sometimes parents do focus on the retarded person in such a way that the rest can feel left out. However, in any family, some function with "longer wings" while others have "shorter wings." There is a normal imbalance concerning how much attention each person needs or gets. It's well worth discussing so no one feels left out.

"He is retarded": *The announcement*

I have known family situations where the announcement came with just as much grief, dramatics, and heaviness as in our story, but no two families take it the same way.

Some take it as a heavy blow. Others see it as a painful announcement that almost instantly brings about a new set of "marching orders" for a family. Sometimes it brings a feeling of wanting to reject the child that is never healed. In any case, it does come as a blow.

Teachers have an excellent opportunity to review how Carla was told and comment on whether it was the best way or if there were other alternatives.

Parents of retarded children have vivid memories of how the professionals told them (another rich point for discussion and comparison) and how they in turn told their children.

"The sound of the word [retarded] made something hurt inside."

There's no doubt about it. Carla—and possibly her parents—were programmed by society to feel that way. S. I. Hayakawa pointed to this fact in a vivid way in a magazine article about Mark, his son with Downs Syndrome.

General semantics deals with the fact that evaluations (value judgments) are built into many of the words we use and that those evaluations govern, and sometimes distort, our thinking: "ex-convict" (don't trust him); "diplomat" (distinguished); "blondes" (have more fun); and, of course, "retarded child" (what a tragedy).

Some parents and teachers have been doing remarkable things to take the frightful negativity out of the word "retarded." Children need to learn from grown-ups that it's not as tragic as it used to be.

Parents, you need to take a look at yourself at this point. It's my hunch Carla wouldn't have taken it as hard as she did if she hadn't picked up the way her parents took it.

69

"Why did it have to happen to us?"

Philosophers and theologians focus on such questions as the basic cry to solve a "specific problem of evil in the world." Tragedy strikes. People cry out. Then they try to find reasons: Was it something they did? Was it in the stars? Is it part of God's plan? Did somebody sin?

It's a funny thing about trying to solve such a problem of evil. When one is in deep travail, the question is raised. Later, when all is calm and relaxed, one forgets to ask the question, and the problem is left unsolved.

Parents and teachers can be extremely helpful with little children at a time like this. Slowly but tenderly they need to help the brothers and sisters to *do some things* that help the family begin to understand, accept, and work with their "shorter winged" brother or sister, as they are able.

Neighbor children and classmates could, within limits, be helpful. Teachers may be in a good position to help their students develop fresh, creative ways of helping. The new spirit of cooperation in our world will begin with such simple actions as these.

"She stopped asking him to go to the drugstore . . .
never visited him in the garden."

Some parents of retarded children confess to a time when they felt repulsed by their retarded child (it would then be understandable that children could feel repulsed, too). They did subtle things to ignore their child. This raises some interesting questions:

- "Is it because we have never learned to live graciously with failure in our own lives?" Failure can make us feel guilty.

- Is it because we have strong needs for stimulating relationships only? Is it hard to give to people who can't give as much in return?

- Is it because our feelings of omnipotence are tested? We like to think we are powerful 'life-changers.' Do we feel helpless when we cannot change our own children into what we want them to be?

- Is it because emotionally we still see retardation as the result of evil? We used to. We say we don't

71

anymore. But, sometimes don't we look at them and wonder if 'somebody sinned'?

● Is it because one of our greatest fears is that we will be found to be stupid and insignificant? Is this one of our most closely guarded fears: that we will be found to be a 'nothing'? (Paul Tillich did write about our fear of nonbeing, you know.)

● Is it because in our particular society we hold high the myth of human progress? We try so hard to believe that man is always making positive development, always moving onward and upward toward achieving the brilliant mind, the beautiful body, and the pure heart which none of us will ever have fully in this life. Maybe we hate to admit that the human process does move backward and downhill at times.

● Or is it more comfortable and secure to keep our relationships confined to those who live, function, and think like ourselves? Can we dare do this when society has now begun to learn that greater creativity comes from struggling with the individual differences of people even if it is risky?

● Notice that the questions raised do not force us to ask, 'What is wrong with persons who are mentally retarded?' Instead, the tables are turned. They force us to ask, 'What is wrong with us and our society that makes us want to avoid those who are mentally retarded?'"*

It is my strong hunch that some persons like Carla would be capable of doing some introspection at this point,

*Robert Perske, *New Directions for Parents of Persons Who Are Retarded* (Nashville: Abingdon Press, 1973), p. 16.

provided the parents and teachers discussed the questions in simple language. For example:

- "I'm so scared of failing, it's hard to have someone around me who does."
- "Can't I do something for people who can't give as much back to me?"
- "I always want to feel big and strong. I'm afraid to be small and weak, so I stay away from those who are."
- "How did I come to see retarded persons as being bad people?"
- "I want to be somebody. Am I afraid others will think I'm a nobody if I'm seen with retarded people?"

Thank goodness for people like Sam at the drugstore.

They can be found in any town! Sometimes they are parents who've been successful in adjusting their family system so their retarded son or daughter is a healthy member-in-full-standing. At other times they are interested citizens who've been involved with retarded persons and their families. At any rate, they've "been there," and they move among us. Furthermore, there are more people like this than we think. A family or a class could make a list of people they know who are like Sam. We may be so busy focusing attention on prejudice that we forget to show gratitude, and we forget to honor those remarkable "attitude changers" who are constantly active among us. Any successful family with a retarded member will be able to name such people.

Small children learn much from adult models. Therefore, it makes good sense to search for persons with

Sam's attitude. You as parents or teachers can develop and be available as models. The same can be said for certain brothers, sisters, neighbors, citizens, and classmates.

"So he taught her his song and together they sang."

Psychologists are quick to tell us that when one does everything possible to solve a human crisis, it is still wrong to assume a certain preferred outcome. But happenings do come! Carla is back with Arthur. She doesn't feel any repulsion or anger just now. Furthermore, Arthur is *teaching her*. This is almost more than one could expect, but sometimes human situations can and do end this way. The solution comes like grace. It's more than we can expect or deserve. It's happenings like these that keep us all growing and developing.

Even young children can be helped to see that the human body and mind have a remarkable ability to reconstitute at a higher level after times of confusion, anxiety, anger, and pain. Parents need to do everything possible to help their children develop such optimism as this. Teachers have the same opportunity. In fact, it would be interesting to help sons, daughters, or classmates to make a list of their "struggles in dark times" and what happened later.

"Mommy and Daddy came out, they . . . smiled at Arthur—who was smiling at Carla—who was smiling at them."

What a beautiful time for reinforcement! Parental response at a time like this makes the victory sweeter.

Some educational psychologists now believe that aversive reinforcement (a fancy name for punishment) may never be needed with some children if the grown-ups around them spend enough time devising innovative but natural ways to recognize, reward, and congratulate their children when they accomplish a new feat. Small children thrive on such positive support as long as it's genuine and not merely a phony attempt to say something nice. The appropriate giving of such rewards becomes a valuable skill.

Furthermore, children can be helped to get the knack of it, too. Arthur will need all the reinforcements for achievements well done he can get from his parents, from Carla, and anyone else who will be able to give them at the appropriate time.

Some Facts to Enhance Discussion

Dr. Phillip Roos, of the National Association for Retarded Citizens, has on many occasions described how chickens have been known to peck to death one of their own who was weak or crippled. He contrasted this with dolphins who have been known to team up, lift one of their weak or injured to the surface for fresh air, and hold that dolphin there for long periods of time. Roos, humorously and forcefully tells us that humankind can be found somewhere on a continuum between a chicken and a dolphin! It is my strong belief that as we help our young to understand and accept mentally retarded brothers, sisters, and playmates, all of us will pay less attention to competitive pecking orders and move toward gracious cooperation epitomized by those remarkable sea-going mammals.

A New Federal Law. They call it the "Education for All Handicapped Children Act," which was passed by the U.S. Congress, November 29, 1975. The Law states:

It is the purpose of this Act to assure that all handicapped children have available to them . . . a free appropriate public education which emphasizes special education and related services designed to meet their unique needs, to assure that the rights of handicapped children and their parents or guardians are protected, to assist States and localities to provide for the education of all handicapped children, and to assess and assure the effectiveness of efforts to educate handicapped children.

Public Law 94-142
(94th Congress, S.6)

Because of this law, more handicapped pupils will be present in public schools. Some schools have already begun projects of "anticipatory planning," helping regular students to be ready to understand, accept, and become involved as helpers and friends. By doing this, negative reactions to their presence can be offset. Planning activities before the fact is much easier than trying to find reactionary solutions, after the fact.

Wouldn't it be great if students and their teachers could do detailed planning for handicapped persons who enter their school; not plans that stem from pity, but genuine attempts to accept them as members in full standing of their portion of the human race. This would amount to true integration with safeguards and supports. Integration without such back-up by teachers and students isn't integration at all. It is "dumping."

Cooperation Instead of Competition. Here's a trend that could be like gold in the lives of persons with handicaps. This is the rationale:

> Students would not be rewarded for competing to see how one can get the most for himself out of education.
>
> Students would be rewarded for their contribution to the achievement of others.

The leader of this trend appears to be Harold Howe II, the former U.S. Commissioner of Education, who is presently vice-president for education and research for the Ford Foundation. In a recent article entitled, "Report to the President of the United States from the Chairman of the White House Conference on Education, August 1, 2024," he stated:

The student who is proficient at reading or mathmatics or who does accurate and high-quality work in the sciences is not necessarily rewarded. The assumption is that he has done well because his particular combination of heredity and environment made that achievement possible. He deserves no recognition for measuring up to his potential. *What the schools increasingly reward is not the student's own achievement but his contribution to the achievement of others.* And the higher

77

his own attainments in learning, the more he is expected to do in helping others to learn.
 —*Saturday Review World,* August 24, 1974

The article goes on to discuss both the hopes and threats in such a trend.

Obviously, Howe and his colleagues have confined their thinking to education in general. But it strikes me that if this trend continues, human beings who happen to have retardation problems in even the so-called severe and profound ranges will feel peer-group assistance and acceptance as never before! Here's a trend we need to watch and assist.

Toward a Fresh Emphasis on the Natural Parent. Now that more people are conscious of the value of early intervention programs, the natural parent is often seen as a key member of the treatment efforts. This is evident in such efforts as:

> *The Portage Project* in which a visiting teacher comes to the home and works with a preschool child on a specific task. She enlists the parent in the task, and the parent takes over. The parent is taught to carry out the daily function and to chart it. The teacher comes back in a week to evaluate and set up a new task.

> *"In-home" residential services.* * A worker goes to the home as soon as possible and poses the question, "What specifically do you need in order for your child to have a full life in your home?" These identified needs are then considered and often provided for the parent *under that family's roof.* It could be an in-home teacher, a baby sitter for the weekend, an automatic washer, or expenses and tutition for a special seminar.

---

*Residential Services Division, Eastern Nebraska Office of Retardation, 116 So. 42nd Street, Omaha, Nebraska 68131.

Visiting Nurses are developing programs where parents are trained under their own roof to carry out infant stimulation programs.

Precision Teaching Programs utilizing "Parent-as-Teacher" methods are being carried out.

Generally, the trend seems to be to:

● Get to the parent early.

● Aid and support the parent as much as possible.

● Do as much as you can under the family roof.

● Do everything possible to assist the parents to work their child into the family system.

By doing so, millions of dollars could be saved on out-of-the-home residential services.

Toward Public Attitude Change. In 1972 at the Montreal meeting of the International League of Societies for the Mentally Handicapped, Phillip Roos lamented that mentally retarded citizens are being successfully programmed to live in the community, but the community was not ready to accept them. He suggested that we work at programs to modify the behavior of the community.

Something stronger than mere "public information" and "public relations" is emerging in one town. There are now programs of planned public attitude change. For example:

● A medical director of an institution near the town had a habit of calling human beings under his care "vegetables."

● A disk jockey made jokes about "the retards" on his radio show.

● A clinician at the Red Cross Blood Bank spoke in dehumanizing terms in front of four young adults formerly from an institution who wanted to give blood for their friend who was dying, but they were denied the chance.

These situations and many more like it were clarified and corrected in this town.

Epilogue

The guide ends here. So much more could be said. I believe that every time a family or community begins to understand a mentally retarded person, we are closer to seeing that:

● Some families—with proper support—will become stronger and richer because a retarded person lives in their midst.

● The true maturity of a nation will depend upon how it accepts and cares for its handicapped.

● Until the so-called normal student attends school with the so-called handicapped, both will be deprived of the best education they could get for living in this world.

● True creative living comes from solving individual differences in relationships.

Now, perhaps the mentally retarded person will be discussed in families and classrooms as never before. Is it wrong to believe that these vital discussions—with skilled leadership—could help create a full life for handicapped persons in the regular flow of community life? And if that happens, all of us will be better for it.

Recommended Resources on Retardation

Organizations

Action for Children's Television
46 Austin Street
Newtonville, Massachusetts 02160

ACT is a national citizens' organization working to facilitate diversity and reduce commercialism in children's television. Serving as a child advocate, ACT encourages television programs that present a positive public image of disabled individuals and promote an attitude of acceptance and inclusion of handicapped youngsters.

ACT published a handbook on programming and children with special needs that serves as a broadcaster's tool for developing programming that enhances the self-concepts and mutual understanding of both handicapped and non-handicapped children.

American Association on Mental Deficiency
5201 Connecticut Avenue
Washington, D.C. 20007

The AAMD, founded in 1876, is a national organization of over 10,000 professionals representing the interests and disciplines dealing with developmental disabilities. The objectives of the association are to effect high standards of programming for the mentally retarded at the community, state, and national levels, and to educate the public to understand and respect retarded persons.

Boy Scouts of America
North Brunswick, New Jersey 08902

Recognizing the need for physical activities for all children, this organization integrates people who are handicapped in regular packs, troops, and posts.

Center on Human Policy
216 Ostrom Avenue
Syracuse, New York 13210

This advocacy organization provides information regarding the legal rights of those with special needs, strategies for change, and community-based programs and services. The center has collated materials on integration, advocacy, and organizing for national distribution.

Closer Look
Box 1492
Washington, D.C. 20013

This national information center is designed to help parents of handicapped children by giving practical advice on finding educational programs and other kinds of special services and resources. Information packets are distributed according to handicapping condition, including possible steps to take to locate services, facts about laws affecting the handicapped, lists of helpful organizations, and suggested readings.

Council for Exceptional Children Information Center
1920 Association Drive
Reston, Virginia 22091

Concerned with the education of handicapped as well as gifted children, the council disseminates abstracts of current research and bibliographies giving a broad overview of topics in publications and nonprint media.

Exceptional Children's Foundation
2225 West Adams Boulevard
Los Angeles, California 90018

The foundation is a multiservice program helping families obtain care and treatment for their retarded children. Programs geared toward the discovery of the retarded individual's potentials and integration into the community include an art center, work training workshops, job preparation and placement, and recreational services.

Girl Scouts of the U.S.A.
Scouting for the Handicapped Girls Program
830 Third Avenue
New York, New York 10022

The Scouting for Handicapped Girls Program is a special effort aimed at making the camp experience of the handicapped girl as much like that of the nonhandicapped girl as possible. Activities include camping, scouting, sports, crafts, service, and learning skills.

Joseph P. Kennedy, Jr., Foundation
1701 K Street, Northwest
Suite 205
Washington, D.C. 20006

The Foundation has worked to determine the causes of mental retardation; to reduce its effects by treatment and training; to promote programs of physical fitness and recreation, such as the Special Olympics; and to make the general public more aware of the needs of retarded persons.

Mental Health Law Project
Suite 300
1220 Nineteenth Street, Northwest
Washington, D.C. 20036

The project, an interdisciplinary public interest organization, is aimed toward protecting the legal rights of individuals who are mentally handicapped and improving conditions of their care, treatment, education, and community living.

Its news letter is published quarterly, describing test-case litigation, legal research, and other activities affecting retarded persons.

National Association of Coordinators of State Programs
for the Mentally Retarded, Inc.
2001 Jefferson Davis Highway
Arlington, Virginia 22202

Concerned with the improvement and expansion of public services to persons who are mentally retarded, the association facilitates the exchange of information about the best methods of providing care and training for retarded persons.

National Association for Retarded Citizens
2709 Avenue E East
Post Office Box 6109
Arlington, Texas 76011

The association is a voluntary nationwide organization providing help to parents, other organizations, and communities in jointly solving problems caused by retardation. Program services include the Child Advocacy Project, residential services, vocational rehabilitation, and the fostering of progresive legislation for retarded persons. On the community level, local NARC units attempt to obtain services for retarded individuals ranging from special classes and preschool programs to sheltered workshops and recreation.

Youth NARC, a national volunteer youth movement, includes young people between the ages of thirteen and twenty-five involved in providing services to mentally retarded individuals and helping create a community awareness and understanding through firsthand experience. Youth NARC also works in public education and governmental affairs.

National Center on Educational Media and Materials
    for the Handicapped
Ohio State University
220 West 12th Avenue
Columbus, Ohio 43210

In conjunction with the national system of learning resource centers, professional associations, and various public and private agencies, the center provides a comprehensive program of activies to facilitate the use of educational technology in instructional programs for handicapped persons.

National Center for Law and the Handicapped, Inc.
1235 North Eddy Street
South Bend, Indiana 46617

The center is designed to insure the legal rights of the handicapped through legal aid, legal and social-science research activities, and programs of public education. Assistance to disabled persons is provided through direct legal intervention and indirectly through consultation with attorneys, organizations, and people involved in litigation. *Amicus*, its bimonthly magazine for both the

84

legal and lay public, covers legal developments relating to the rights of the handicapped.

Physical Education and Recreation for the Handicapped Information and Research Utilitation Center American Alliance for Health, Physical Education, and Recreation
Room 422
1201 16th Street
Washington, D.C. 20036

This comprehensive center provides information and materials about all aspects of physical education and related areas for impaired, disabled, and handicapped persons.

President's Committee on Employment of the Handicapped
Washington, D.C. 20210

The committee consists of over 600 organizations and individuals representing a cross section of America: business, labor, professions, rehabilitation, youth, and other groups. The organization is devoted to creating an atmosphere of acceptance that would allow handicapped individuals to have their full share of opportunities to work. Handicapped persons may also use the committee as a sounding board. The committee has published a series of helpful, informative pamphlets describing the different kinds of barriers the handicapped encounter in their daily living, and the ways such barriers can be eliminated.

President's Committee on Mental Retardation
Washington, D.C. 20201

The committee advises the President in evaluating the national effort to prevent mental retardation; acts as a liaison between the federal government and public and private agencies; and releases public information to improve the conditions for retarded individuals. The committee also publishes a series of pamphlets dealing with different aspects of mental retardation.

Special Education Resource Center
275 Windsor Street
Hartford, Connecticut 06120

Designed to serve professionals, parents, and college students, the center offers instructional materials, consultative services, and periodic workshops and presentations related to the dissemination of information about educational materials for exceptional children.

Further Reading

Preschool to Age 8

Brightman, Alan, *Like Me* (Boston: Little, Brown, and Company, 1976).
  Through text and colored photographs, young readers learn that while retarded children may be slower with some things, they are like you and me in their desire to succeed and their need to have friends.

Doorly, Ruth, *Our Jimmy* (Westwood, Massachusetts: Service Associates, 1967).
  The father in the story explains why Jimmy, a mentally retarded boy, needs special consideration and in turn, how he contributes to the happiness of the family. Especially helpful for siblings of retarded children.

Fassler, Joan, *One Little Girl* (New York: Behavioral Publications, Inc., 1969).
  Grown-ups call Laurie a slow child which makes Laurie feel very sad. Then she discovers that while she may be slow in doing some things, she can do others just as well as other people.

Guggenheim, Hans, *The World of Wonderful Difference* (New York: Friendly House Publishers, 1960).
  Verse and delightful illustrations show the value of differences among people.

Lasker, Joe, *He's My Brother* (Chicago: Albert Whitman and Co., 1974).
A young boy's description of the experiences of his slow learning brother at school and at home.

Middle Grades, Ages 8 – 11

Christopher, Matt, *Long Shot for Paul* (Boston: Little, Brown, and Company 1966).
A story of a boy's determination to make his mentally retarded brother a good basketball player and valuable member of the team.

Gardner, Richard, *MBD: Family Book of Minimal Brain Damage* (New York: Jason Aronson, 1973).
An informative book for children and their parents about minimal brain damage.

Grealish, Charles, and Mary Jane VonBraunsberg, *Amy Maura* (Syracuse, New York: Human Policy Press, 1975).
A story about a young girl and her self-concept. The question is, will others accept her with a disability?

Klein, Gerda, *The Blue Rose* (New York: Lawrence Hill and Co., 1974).
Brief poetic text and black-and-white photographs explain how Jenny is different and why she needs more love and understanding.

Little, Jean, *Take Wing* (Boston: Little, Brown and Co., 1968).
Laurel struggles to make friends with other children while protecting her mentally retarded brother.

Smith, Gene, *Hay Burners* (New York: Delacorte Press, 1974).
To young Will, the steer which he has been assigned to raise seems to be a loser. Joey, a mentally retarded farmhand, through his love and care for the animal, teaches Will a lesson.

Ages 11–13

Bradbury, Bianca, *Nancy and Her Johnny-O* (New York: Washburn Ives, Inc. 1970).
An adolescent girl relates to her young brother who is mildly retarded in various ways.

Byars, Betsy, *The Summer of Swans* (New York: Viking Press, 1970).
Eighth-grade Sara, shy and sensitive, tries to protect her retarded younger brother.

Carpelan, Bo, *Bow Island* (New York: Delacorte Press, 1971).
During the summer holiday in a fisherman's cottage, 12-year-old John tries to protect 19-year-old Marvin, who is mentally retarded, from the cruel attacks of other children.

Cleaver, Vera and Bill, *Me Too* (Philadelphia: J. B. Lippincott, 1973).
Lydia's father leaves home and her mother has to work, so the 12-year-old girl is left to look after her retarded twin sister during the summer. Lydia tries desperately to teach Lornie and to win some expression of love.

Crane, Caroline, *Girl Like Tracy* (New York: David McKay Publishing Company, 1966).
With a mentally retarded older sister needing constant protection, and her parents incapable of handling the situation, Kathy despairs until a teacher shows a partial solution.

Friis-Baastad, Babbis, *Don't Take Teddy* (New York: Charles Scribner's Sons, 1967).
A first-person account of young Mikkel's confused feelings about Teddy, his retarded brother. They run away, to escape the possible consequences of Teddy's wrongdoing—a journey leading to Mikkel's acceptance of his brother's disability.

Koob, Theodore, *Deep Search* (Philadelphia: J. B. Lippincott, 1969).
A young girl is confused when her parents disagree about the future of her 10-year-old mentally retarded brother.

Luis, Earlene W., and Barbara Miller. *Listen Lissa* (New York: Dodd, Mead, and Company, 1968).
The story portrays both the difficulties and joys of a family with an 11-year-old boy who is severely retarded.

Platt, Kin, *Hey Dummy* (Philadelphia: Chilton Book Company, 1971).
Twelve-year-old Neil befriends Alan, a brain-damaged boy of thirteen. Neil's involvement grows deeper as he comes to understand Alan's plight in the midst of cruel taunting from his peers and the outrage of Neil's frightened parents.

Reynolds, Pamela, *A Different Kind of Sister* (New York: Lothrop, Lee, and Shepard Company, 1968).
A story about a 13-year-old girl and her relationship with her 18-year-old retarded sister, who has returned home after living in an institution for four years.

Wrightson, Patricia, *Racecourse for Andy* (New York: Harcourt, Brace, Jovanovich, Inc., 1968).
When Andy, who is not quite like other boys, buys a racehorse for three dollars, his friends rally to support him.

Ages 13 and Up

Biklen, Douglas, *Let Our Children Go, An Organizing Manual for Parents and Advocates* (Syracuse, New York: Human Policy Press, 1974).
Describes how parents of children with disabilities and their allies can fight for their own needs and rights. A manual for action and change, it details the basic steps to successful advocacy organizing.

Blatt, Burton, and Fred Kaplan, *Christmas in Purgatory, A Photographic Essay on Mental Retardation* (Syracuse, New York: Human Policy Press, 1974).
A startling photo essay of legally sanctioned human abuse in state institutions.

Hunt, Nigel, *The World of Nigel Hunt* (New York: Garrett Publishers, 1967).
A heartwarming autobiography by a young man with Down's Syndrome.

Hurwitz, Howard, *Donald, the Man Who Remains a Boy* (New York: Simon and Schuster, 1973).
A father's first-person account of his family's determination to raise Donald, their retarded son, at home. This true story reveals thirty years of the seemingly unendurable pain and the special joys of their life together.

Keyes, Daniel, *Flowers for Algernon* (New York: Harcourt, Brace, Jovanovich, Inc., 1966).
A sensitive novel about a retarded man who miraculously, through an experiment, journeys into the world of normality.

Man, Abby, *A Child Is Waiting* (New York: Popular Library, 1963).
A teacher's stereotyped conceptions of her retarded students fade as she comes to recognize them as very special individuals.

Murray, Dorothy, *This Is Stevie's Story* (Nashville: Abingdon Press, 1967).
A mother's true story of how she raised a son who was mentally retarded.

Perske, Robert, *New Directions for Parents of Persons Who are Retarded* (Nashville: Abingdon Press, 1973).
This sensitive book deals honestly with the pains, fears, and hopes of parents of retarded children.

Roberts, Bruce and Nancy, *David* (Richmond, Virginia: John Knox Press, 1968).
Through photographs and narrative one learns about David, a young boy with Down's Syndrome, at home and in his community.

Steinbeck, John, *Of Mice and Men* (New York: Bantam, 1937).
Classic novel about the friendship between two rootless workers in California: Lennie, who is brain damaged as a result of an accident, and George, who acts as Lennie's protector.

Wexler, Susan Stanhope, *The Story of Sandy* (New York: Bobbs-Merril Co., Inc., 1955).
The true story of a foster parent who refuses to believe her little boy is hopelessly retarded.

Public Affairs Pamphlets

The nonprofit Public Affairs Committee (381 Park Avenue South, New York, New York 10016) publishes excellent resource aids in the following concise, informative, and inexpensive booklets:

How Retarded Children Can Be Helped (No. 288)
Evelyn Hart disproves popular fallacies regarding individuals who are retarded as she describes how they can be helped through community services.

Independent Living: New Goal for Disabled Persons (No. 522)
What are the handicapped person's alternatives to living in an institution? This question is explored and practical answers are given.

New Hope for the Retarded Child (No. 210A)
Dr. Walter Jacob explains what mental retardation is, what are its causes and steps in diagnosis, and finally, what citizens can do to help individuals who are handicapped.

The Retarded Child Gets Ready for School (No. 349)
Margaret Hill, education chairman of the Wyoming state branch of the national Association for Retarded Citizens, discusses the various strategies and methods in teaching retarded children.

Securing the Legal Rights of Retarded Persons (No. 492)
This informative and readable pamphlet deals with the retarded person's legal rights to education, treatment, and place in the community.

National Association for Retarded Citizens Pamphlets

Many helpful brochures dealing with various aspects of mental retardation may be obtained from the National Association for Retarded Citizens, 2709 Avenue East, POB 6109, Arlington, Texas 76011. Among them are the following:

Facts on Mental Retardation
Answers are given to the most frequently asked questions

about mental retardation: causes, prevention, and steps
required to meet the needs of the retarded.

Citizen Advocacy Is Something Shared
This small brochure provides a brief overview of the Citizen
Advocacy concept.

To Our Children's Children; Prevention Handbook
This practical handbook focuses on fifteen major pre-
ventable causes of mental retardation and provides steps
for prevention programs.

Avenues to Change, a four-part series, is highly useful in imple-
menting citizen advocacy programs.

Part I) *Citizen Advocacy for Mentally Retarded Children: An
Introduction*
Describes the various roles of the citizen advocate and
examines the structure of the Citizen Advocacy program.

(Part II) *Implementation of Citizen Advocacy Through State
and Local ARCs*
Designed for program staff, Part II is a a step-by-step guide to
the implementation and operation of a Citizen Advocacy
program.

(Part III) *Effective Advocacy*
A handbook for advocates, Part III proposes possible activities for the advocates and their retarded friends and gives
suggestions for dealing with the different phases of their
relationship.

(Part IV) *Youth as a Citizen Advocate*
Deals with teenagers and their relationships with people who
are classified as retarded.

Siblings of the Retarded
Practical suggestions are given for handling problems of the
brothers and sisters of retarded children.

The Mentally Handicapped Child Under Five
Gunnar Dybwad describes the services and support needed
to adequately handle the problems of the family with a
young retarded child.

Other Printed Resources

The Exceptional Parent
  Box 964, Manchester, New Hampshire 03105.
    This magazine, published six times yearly, is designed for
    parents of children with special needs.

Please Know Me as I Am: A Guide to Helping Children Understand the Child With Special Needs
  Massachusetts State Plan for Services and Facilities for the
  Developmentally Disabled.
    Margaret Cleary's comprehensive resource guide is especially
    useful for adults in helping their children better understand
    their companions with special needs.

Resource Materials for Serving Those with Special Needs
  Massachusetts Department of Mental Health, Division of Mental
  Retardation, Media Resource Center, Box 158, Belmont,
  Massachusetts 02178.
    This excellent catalogue contains a wealth of resources about
    the needs of people who are handicapped, including films
    and books for all ages.

Films

Recommended Films for Younger Children

How Do You Feel?
  20 minutes, color. Massachusetts Department of Mental Health,
  Division of Mental Retardation, Media Resource Center, Box
  158, Belmont, Massachusetts 02178.
    Through a series of interviews, one learns that all people,
    disabled or not, share similiar feelings.

Meet Lisa
  5 minutes, color. Boston University Film Library, 765 Commonwealth Avenue, Boston, Massachusetts 02215.
    Lisa is a brain-injured child. Like other children, she needs
    love and acceptance. The film presents Lisa's world as she
    grows and learns in her own special way.

Patrick
6 minutes, color. Massachusetts Association for Retarded
Citizens, 381 Elliot Street, Newton Upper Falls, Massachusetts
02164.
A sensitive film portraying Patrick, a retarded boy of eight,
and his relationship with his brother and sister.

The Point
75 minutes, color, animated, MacMillan Audio Brandon, 34
MacQueston Parkway South, Mount Vernon, New York
10550.
An enchanting fantasy about an unusual kingdom in which
everything is pointed except for a young boy named Oblio.
He learns through his adventures that it is not at all necessary
to be pointed to have a point in life. It is okay to be different.

The Purple Adventures of Lady Elaine Fairchilde
A nonbroadcast package consisting of five half-hour video
cassettes drawn from past Mister Rogers' Neighborhood seg-
ments is available from: Family Communications, Inc., 4802
Fifth Avenue, Pittsburgh, Pennsylvania 15213.
The story places a high value on individual differences. The
many ways of being different are considered such as age,
sex, and race, as well as being disabled, yet without emphasizing the idea of being handicapped. This approach
makes the series especially appropriate for integrated settings.

A Walk in Another Pair of Shoes
18½ minutes, color. CANHC Film Distributors, POB 604, Main
Office, Los Angeles, California 90053.
The filmstrip illustrates how it feels to be a child with learning
disabilities by showing the problems encountered by children
with special needs.

What Would You Do?—On Being Left Out
10 minutes, color. Massachusetts Department of Mental Health,
Division of Mental Retardation, Media Resource Center, Box 158,
Belmont, Massachusetts 02178.
The slide tape helps children understand the differences and
similarities of all people.

For Older Youth

Charly
103 minutes, color. Films Inc., 1144 Wilmette Avenue,
Wilmette, Illinois 60091.
Film production based on Daniel Keyes' sensitive novel,
Flowers for Algernon. Charly, a thirty-year-old man with the
mental capabilities of a six-year-old, achieves normality after
experimentation in a mental retardation clinic only to learn
he will soon revert to his former state.

*Children Learn Together: The Integration of Handicapped
Children into Schools*
132 slides, color. Human Policy Press, POB 127, University
Station, Syracuse, New York 13210.
Ellen Barnes' slide show deals with "mainstreaming," the
integration of handicapped children into schools. Discussion
presents what is necessary for integration to succeed, as well
as the history of the segration of disabled children.
Included are a script accompanying each slide and a com-
plete bibliography on mainstreaming.

Citizen Advocacy: An Answer for Thursday's Child
12 minutes, color. NARC, 2079 Avenue E East, POB 6109,
Arlington, Texas 76011.
The slide presentation with accompanying tape-recorded
script is designed as a training tool for citizen advocates as it
describes the variety of advocate roles as friend, tutor, or
adoptive parent.

Come and Get to Know Me
10 minutes, color. Massachusetts Department of Mental Health,
Division of Mental Retardation, Media Resource Center, Box 158,
Belmont, Massachusetts 02178.
The slide-tape presentation encourages a better understanding
of and a greater sensitivity toward people with handicaps.
Various people and programs are shown, to the accompani-
ment of four original songs by Dana Wells.

The Community and the Exceptional Child
30 minutes, black and white. Kent State University, Audio
Visual Services, Kent, Ohio 44242.
Dr. William Cruickshank reviews the common problems faced

by parents, the school, and the community at large in fulfilling their responsibilities to the exceptional child.

Greene Valley Grandparents
10 minutes, black and white, University of Michigan, Audio-Visual Education Center, 416 Fourth Street, Ann Arbor, Michigan 48103.
Retired people who work with mentally retarded children at the Greene Valley Developmental Center comment throughout the film on what the program means to them and to the children.

Growth Failure and Maternal Deprivation
28 minutes, black and white. McGraw-Hill Films, 330 West 42nd Street, New York, New York 10022.
Physical and mental retardation in young children may often result from lack of parental attention. This documentary is aimed at prevention as it demonstrates the aspects of the mother-child relationship thought to be responsible for failure of some children to grow and develop normally.

Individual Differences, Introduction
29 minutes, black and white. Indiana University, Audio-Visual Center, Bloomington, Indiana 47401.
The film explains that individual differences in children occur in physical, mental, and emotional growth and development, and describes the special problems of the exceptional child.

Kris: A Family Portrait
18 minutes, color. Ithaca College, School of Communications, Ithaca, New York 14850.
Kris is 18 years old. The film starts with his birth and the discovery that he is blind and mentally retarded, and traces the relationships with his mother, father, and older brother to the present time.

Larry
78 minutes, color. University of California, Extension Media Center, Berkeley, California 94720.
Larry is a young man of normal intelligence who was thought to be mentally retarded and was institutionalized from early childhood. This moving drama traces his struggle to adapt to the normal world with the assistance of a perceptive and sensitive woman psychologist.

Like Other People
   37 minutes, color. Boston University Film Library, 765 Commonwealth Avenue, Boston, Massachusetts 02215.
   The film examines the emotional and social needs of handicapped individuals.

Lisa's World
   30 minutes, color. University of Michigan, Audio-Visual Education Center, 416 Fourth Street, Ann Arbor, Michigan 48103.
   The life of a family with a mildly retarded 7-year-old girl is recounted, revealing the difficulties and rewards of raising the child in the normal home setting and the effect on other members of the family.

The Long Childhood of Timmy
   53 minutes, black and white. McGraw-Hill Films, 330 West 42nd Street, New York, New York 10022.
   The film presents the lives of the Loughlins and the relationships and feelings which develop as a result of 9-year-old Timmy's retardation.

Of Mice and Men
   110 minutes, black and white. McGraw-Hill Films, 330 West 42nd Street, New York, New York 10022.
   The screen version of John Steinbeck's classic novel protrays the tragic and strange friendship of two ranch hands, one of whom is brain injured as a result of an accident.

Parent Advocacy: An Interview with Robert Perske
   30 minutes. Massachusetts Department of Mental Health, Division of Mental Retardation, Media Resource Center, Box 158, Belmont, Massachusetts 02178.
   Robert Perske, past director of the Greater Omaha Association for Retarded Citizens, discusses advocacy programs.

Something Shared
   15 minutes, color. NARC, 2708 Avenue E East, Arlington, Texas 76010.
   The film illustrates the relationships between citizen advocates and developmentally disabled persons.

Stress: Parents with a Handicapped Child
   30 minutes, black and white. McGraw-Hill Films, 330 West 42nd Street, New York, New York 10022.

Going directly into the homes of five families with handicapped children, candid shots present the facts and let them speak for themselves.

They Call Me Names
22 minutes, color. BFA Educational Media, 22111 Michigan Avenue, Santa Monica, California 90404.

How does it feel to be different from those around you? The film portrays the lives of mentally different young people and explores how they perceive a world in which they are told often and in many ways that they are different.

Those Other Kids
26 minutes, color. Indiana University, Audio-Visual Center, Bloomington, Indiana 47401.

This documentary film reviews the history of educational rights for the handicapped and explains the impact of the recent court rulings asserting that all students, including the handicapped, have a right to equal educational opportunities.

Where the Children Are: A Slide Show on Institutions and Alternatives
129 slides, color. Human Policy Press, POB 127, University Station, Syracuse, New York 13210.

Douglas Biklen's report describes how institutions developed, what they are like inside, and how we can change them. The Child Advocacy movement, its strategies, and its progress are discussed. The program focuses on efforts to integrate people with disabilities into community settings.

The show includes a script with text accompanying each slide and a bibliography.

A World of the Right Size
21 minutes, color. Nebraska Psychological Institute, Communications Division, 602 South 44th Avenue, Omaha, Nebraska 68105.

This cartoon-film presents an overview of the nature of mental retardation, emphasizing that the retarded child should be accepted as an individual with his unique potentials and limitations.